This Little Book Belongs to:

_____

_____

Dedicated to my Dad

Stardust & Love, 2020
Series: Little Books for Little Warriors Volume 3
Written and illustrated by Jessycka Drew

Copyright © 2020 Jessycka Drew
All rights reserved.
MotherButterfly Books
www.motherbutterfly.com

This edition is published by arrangement with Jessycka Drew.
All Rights Reserved. No part of this publication may be reproduced or transmitted in any form or by any means, electronic or mechanical, including photocopying, recording, or any information storage and retrieval systems, without permission in writing from the publisher.

Requests for permission to make copies of any part of this work should be submitted online at www.motherbutterfly.com

ISBN 978-1-989579-05-3

www.motherbutterfly.com
laugh.learn.love

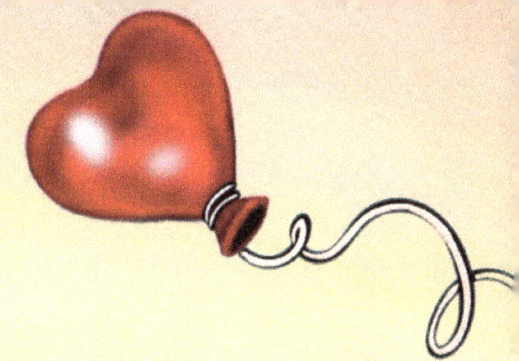

Stardust & Love

From The Imaginative World of Jessycka Drew

Greetings Dear One, from Jessycka Drew.
I write little books with messages to YOU!
My little books are to give you some help
with all sorts of things that may come about!

This little book is to help you through
the loss of someone dear to you.
From the bottom of my heart and written with care,
a message of hope is what I will share.

What do you do
when you learn the news
that you've lost someone
very special to you?

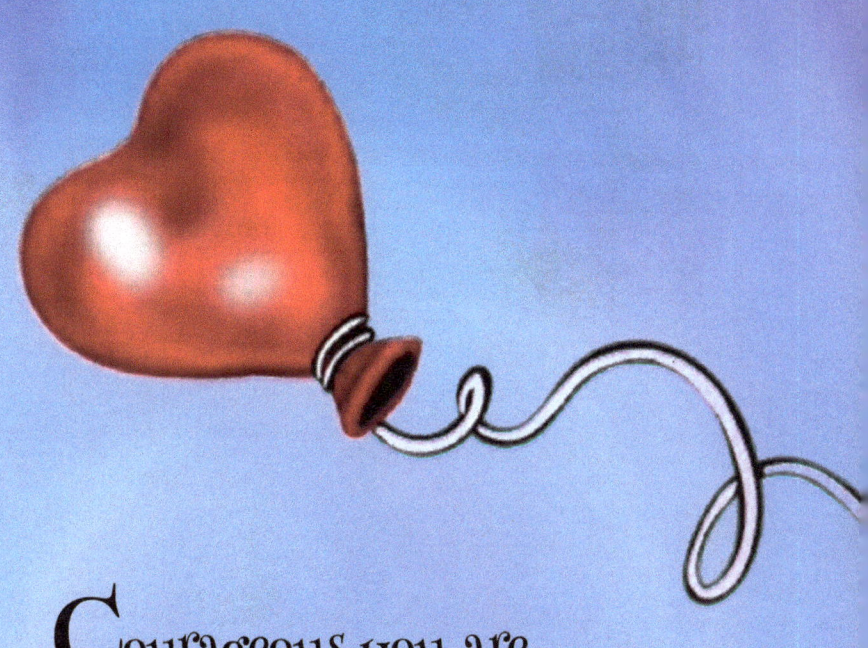

Courageous you are,
yes you, Dear One,
you are facing tough stuff,
that's not at all fun!

When all of a sudden you have been forced to part from someone near and dear to your heart...

You can gather the pieces together and start to heal the hurt in your very big heart.

Understanding a loss
is no easy task.
So many questions
to yourself you may ask...
Where did they go?
Why did they leave?
Is it something I did?
I wish I could see...

It's important for you
to know, my Dear One,
It's not your fault
if you've lost someone.

There's something, my Dear One, that you must know, about what we are and where we go.

Everyone, including you and me...

Are made up of stardust, love, and energy!

We never die
in the way you may think.
We are sailing a ship
that doesn't ever sink.

This very life
is a wave we are on.
We ride together,
we sing the same song!

Sometimes our being, of love and stardust, changes its tune and go we must! This doesn't mean we go to a place with nothing but empty space.

No, no, Dear One,
they just changed their tune.
I know it seems
like it happens too soon...
But still, made up of energy they are,
And full of love and dust from a star!

Just like you and me, my dear,
Lost they are not, their energy is near!

They are still with you,
still right by your side.
They caught the next wave,
which they now ride.

They aren't far away, not far at all.

You can say hello still,

give them a call...

How do you know when your loved one hears you?

Well, you see the wave they transitioned to...

Is everything and everywhere,
it's in the ocean and in the air.

When you think of your loved one,
and feel the wind blow,
or you see the leaves rustle,
that's how you know!

Remember?

I told you what we are made of,
energy, stardust, and of course, love!
When you see the stars
and they twinkle at you...

The Moon smiles at you
from way up in the sky,
That's just them again
keeping an eye!

Ask for their help
and know they are there
when you feel that prickly feeling...
Yes, that right there!
You know what I mean,
when your hair stands on end?
That's the tickling message they send!

When you're hurting, or sad, or scared my Dear One, Remember your loved one is never really gone...

The wave of life is quite a ride,
Ups and downs flow like the tide.
If someone you love
starts singing to you
and you hear a song
on the wave next to you...

Greet them with
the windy breeze,
Say HELLO
with the rustling leaves.

Smile at the Moon
as it keeps an eye,
wink at the stars
in the twinkling sky!

My Dear,
you must know
that you are never alone.
Every battle you face,
no matter how grown,
you stand surrounded
by the loved ones you thought...
were gone, but Dear One,
remember they're not!

LOVE lasts forever
and that's what we are!
Beings of love and dust
from each star!

YOU, my dear friend,
are more than you know,
you shimmer with love.
Look how you glow!!

You are strong, courageous,
and of course, brave too,
I'm just so unbelievably
inspired by you!

The energy of love
and stardust too,
is infinite you know,
and so are YOU!

When you are feeling sad, angry, or blue,
look into the mirror and say this to YOU!
Repeat this over and over to you...
Because it is so unbelievably true!
READY?!
Are you looking directly at you?!
Don't be shy...
Here we go!

Mirror Mirror on the Wall

You, my dear,
are so much more than you know,
You shimmer with love,
just look how you glow!

You are strong and courageous
and brave too,
I am so unbelievably
inspired by you!

You Are Beautiful!

If you have lost someone
dear to your heart,
And you're having trouble
being so far apart,
there is a way to get
a message through
to someone that's
oh so far from you!

Send a message in a bottle,
or a message in a jar,
Write down your special message
and it will go quite far.

You can send your message with the sea,
Or keep your messages at home to be
Sent out from the bottle
or jar with love
and with a prayer
to reach the oceans above,
to reach the very one
you lost one day
but still have so much
you have to say!

DECORATE:
A bottle, jar, or container.

GATHER:
Paper and a pen.

WRITE:
Messages and place them inside.

SEND OFF WITH LOVE:
Say or write this little prayer...

May my message reach

the ocean up above,

I send this note with

stardust,

energy,

and love!

The language of the universe, energy and love
is how those communicate from the oceans above!

"Hello!" from the other side

Loved ones you've lost
can communicate with you,
Signs, hints, and messages
come through to you.

So,
LISTEN,
LOOK,
FEEL
around, my dear,
For the world around you
is how they speak
...do you hear?

Clouds, feathers, a penny, oh my!
How many ways will they try
to say HELLO to YOU my Dear?
Are you LISTENING? Do you HEAR?

The windy breeze, rustling leaves
could be HELLO to YOU! Do you SEE?

The moon can wink,
the stars can guide,
the messages from above
will not hide.

You just have be aware,
and LOOK,
and LISTEN,
and FEEL what's there!

Loved this Book?

Sharing is Caring!

Please share the love by leaving a review online.

THANK YOU for helping to share our books with families around the world!

GoodReads
Amazon
Indigo
Barnes and Noble
iBooks
Google Play
Kobo

laugh.learn.love
MotherButterfly.com

GO TO:

motherbutterfly.com/littlewarriors

for your FREE book!

www.ingramcontent.com/pod-product-compliance
Lightning Source LLC
Chambersburg PA
CBHW061732070526
44583CB00024B/3105